STOP COMPLAINING: START THANKING!

Published by:
Gita Publishing House
Sadhu Vaswani Mission,
10, Sadhu Vaswani Path,
Pune 411 001, (India).
gph@sadhuvaswani.org
www.dadavaswanisbooks.org

Second Edition

ISBN : 978-93-80743-31-8

Printed by:
Mehta Offset Pvt. Ltd.
Mehta House,
A-16, Naraina Industrial Area II,
New Delhi 110 028, (India).
Phone : +91-11-45670222
info@mehtaoffset.com

STOP COMPLAINING: START THANKING!

J.P. Vaswani

Gita Publishing House
Pune, (India).
www.dadavaswanisbooks.org

Other Books By Dada J.P. Vaswani

PREFACE

Thank you God! Thank you God! Thank you God!

Rev. Dada J. P. Vaswani tells us that this *mantra* is his favourite form of communication with the Lord. According to Dada, the words "Thank you!" have a magical quality about them. There is music, melody, sunshine and warmth in them. Utter these words to yourself; try and say them with a smile, for added effect – and you will find that you are filled with the energy of positive vibrations and the vitalising power of gratitude!

When we say "Thank you!" to our friends and colleagues and family members, let us not simply make it lip-service. When uttered with genuine feelings, these magical words can help us win friends, sustain and promote better relationships and take us on the path that changes mere living into the fine art of living with joy and grace!

How can we live and work in the beautiful spirit of grateful acceptance that makes our life an unending song of love and joy and peace? How can we learn to cherish our friends and win over the hearts and minds of our loved ones? How can we make the most of this precious life which is God's greatest gift to us?

On the joyous occasion of Thanksgiving Week, 2011, we offer you Rev. Dada's beautiful new book, with its central message ringing clear and fine in the title: Stop Complaining, Start Thanking!

Make this the motto of your life, and see your life transformed!

CONTENTS

There Is So Much To Be Grateful For!

> **If the only prayer you said in your life was "thank you", that would suffice.**
>
> *—Meister Eckhart*

Thank you God! Thank you God! Thank you God!

*F*riends who have heard me speak or read any of my books know that this is my favourite form of communication with God. In sunshine and rain, in pleasure and pain, in loss and gain, in darkness and light, this is a prayer that I love to offer to God. I say this to Him in all circumstances and all events of life. I say it with the fullest confidence that whatever is happening to me at that moment, is a gift, *prasadam* from His spotless hands.

As I said to you, this is my favourite prayer: but many of the brothers and sisters with whom I have shared this prayer are not convinced by my poor words. "Thank God?" they ask, incredulous with anger and frustration. "Thank God? For what? For inflation and recession? For debts and mounting bills? For the cruelty and indifference we meet wherever we turn? For illness and pain?"

I say to them with a smile, "I am not one of those cruel, indifferent people you are talking about! I know that life is not always smooth sailing for us human beings. But I do know, that God is all love and all wisdom. He is too loving to punish and too wise to make a mistake. Whatever is happening to you must be for your own good – though you may not be aware of it when it is happening. Therefore, I say to you, let the words, 'Thank you God! Thank you God! Thank you God!' be on your lips constantly! A grateful heart will make your life beautiful and abundantly blessed!"

As for that question, "What is there to be grateful about?" I must confess that it leaves me speechless with disbelief! What is there that I need not be grateful for – is my response. As for me, I am grateful to be alive; I am grateful that I can see and hear and feel; let me add for your sake: you must be grateful that you can walk and run. As for me, after six months of enforced rest, I am beginning to take 'baby' steps after a complicated orthopaedic surgery and consequent stroke, and let me say, I am profoundly grateful that I can come to the *satsang* and meet my brothers and sisters. I would be an ungrateful person, if I did not express my gratitude to the doctors, nurses, physiotherapists and the numerous brothers and sisters who sent out their prayers for my recovery. I cannot, at present, walk without help; as for running, it is out of question; but I am grateful that I am still moving despite the pain and the difficulty!

There! I began with a list of things you ought to be grateful for, and I was forced to point out to you that these are things that some of us cannot take for granted! But let me continue with your gratitude list: you can speak; you can eat; you can smell; you can laugh and cry; you can add and subtract; you can read and understand; you can sing and dance. Should I go on...?

The trouble with many of us is that we only focus on what we do not have, and forget all that we have been blessed with. This attitude makes for ingratitude.

Is it not true that many of us just go through life always wanting something or the other, always complaining that this or that is lacking in our lives, homes and offices? Young ladies who are short, want to be taller; young men who are thin want to become muscular; people with straight hair want curly hair; and everyone with an Indian complexion wants an European complexion. Nobody is satisfied; nobody is happy; everyone wants to be something which he or she is not; how can we even begin to be grateful for what we have?

The trouble is that in this mad race of wanting what we do not have, many of us overlook what we have to be thankful for. In fact, we take for granted so many precious things that make our lives worth living.

Where would we be without our families? What would we do if we had no homes to go back to at the end of the day? It is a different thing that all of us want bigger, better homes, may be with greater amenities and luxuries. But have you ever thought what it is like to be homeless?

May I say to you, every year, year after year, in the cold season of winter, our Sadhu Vaswani Mission volunteers go out to offer blankets to people who sleep on the pavements of Pune. These people live and eat and sleep on the pavements. Some actually live with their children, cooking and cleaning and running a home on the pavement, until the authorities come along and 'demolish' their homes in a few seconds! The other day, a sister said to me that the makeshift homes of twenty pavement-dweller-families had been displaced from the station area, and they were all wailing loudly by the roadside. A few hours later, they had packed their belongings and moved on! They could not afford the luxury of endless complaining. They had to make alternative arrangements.

Believe me, when you stop complaining and start thanking, when you stop criticising and start appreciating, your life will be transformed! You will find yourself living a rich, meaningful, worthwhile life, which is filled with abundance and a source of joy and peace to yourself and those around you!

Try the attitude of gratitude. And see the difference for yourself!

The Attitude Of Gratitude

Gratitude is not only the greatest of virtues, but a parent of all the others.

—Cicero

*W*hy should I be grateful? Most of the world's scriptures and nearly all the world's great spiritual masters emphasise that gratitude is essential for the life beautiful. Most ordinary people too, would agree that complaining and criticising can make life bitter and sour – and bitterness and sourness, as we know, are not anybody's 'flavours-of-the-week!' Being grateful makes us positive, happy and optimistic; it helps us see the bright side of life. It teaches us the art of appreciation, which, I am afraid, is becoming a lost art for some of us today.

Some experts believe that we lack in the spirit of gratitude because we take things for granted. The street urchin into whose hands you drop a packet of biscuits looks up at you with gratitude and smiles happily. He has known what it is to be hungry, to go without food oftentimes. He knows the value of those biscuits which may not be dainty enough for our palates. What do we do? Someone takes the trouble to shop and plan and cook and clean, so that a plate of hot food is put before us at regular intervals; we make faces and complain that the dish is either too spicy or not spicy enough; that it is boring; that it is not our favourite recipe that has been served; and that the vegetables on the plate are not the ones we like!

May be we need to go without the things we take for granted, to be able to appreciate what we have.

Now give me one good reason why we should allow that to happen? Why should we allow ourselves to go through a loss just to realise the value of what we already have?

When you become aware of all that you have to be grateful for, when you actually begin to count your blessings, you will be overwhelmed with gratitude for all that God has bestoweed on you so unstintingly. Your peaceful sleep, your loved ones whose dearest wish is just to see you happy, your friends who add value to your life, your good health which you utterly fail to appreciate until you fall ill, the fresh air and sunlight around you, the marvels of technology which have made your life so easy, the society and community which lets you live in peace and order – where would you be without them all?

Gratitude is the foundation of a peaceful life, a secure and stable mind; it is also the essence of spirituality.

Many people think that if they had a little more of this or that, a little more than what they now have, they would indeed be very happy, satisfied and thankful: they are quite mistaken. If we are not satisfied with what we have, we are not likely to be satisfied even if it were increased many times!

On his first posting, a missionary travelled to Uganda. He was surprised to see that most men he met there, had just two shirts. He was taken aback by this and asked his guide why this was so. The guide said simply, "When one gets dirty, they wash it, while the second one is worn."

If you are one of those people who stand before your open wardrobe and take close to ten minutes to decide what you will wear today, ask yourself: don't you owe a debt of gratitude to God for all that you have?

Have you heard of the law of attraction? Put quite simply, it is this: what you feel strongly about, happens to you. It is that thought power that I often speak of, which makes things happen. If you feel grateful for what you have, you will attract many more things to be grateful for. Gratitude is the very basis of the abundant law of attraction.

I often urge my dissatisfied friends to actually put down in black and white, all the things for which they are truly grateful: they are in a black mood while they struggle to think of the first two or three; and then, the joy of discovering gratitude carries them forward, and they often go effortlessly up to one hundred things/people/gifts for which they are grateful. They keep going and simply don't want to stop. Their very attitude changes for the better, and they find that their whole life is put in a new perspective.

Would you like to try this energising exercise? Try and write down all that you should be grateful for. Do not leave out anything! Do not take anything or anyone for granted!

Being alive, being free to do what you care about, being literate, being with people – these are not rights for all; they are privileges which we enjoy and take for granted. And we ought to be grateful for them.

But we must remember that gratitude is not an attitude to yourself; it should be an attitude to life, an attitude which you show to others. Gratitude is most beautiful when it is expressed, and not just when it is felt. How can we feel gratitude without showing it? How can we show gratitude without sharing it, expressing it to others? When we show gratitude, when we express gratitude, we are sharing our joy and happiness with others. In the Hindu way of prayer, we light *agarbattis* or offer incense to show our gratitude to God; the fragrance from the incense spreads all around, making others happy. So it is with gratitude: it blesses both the giver and the receiver. It strengthens their faith in life, and teaches them to show their gratitude to others.

The Secret Of
Successful Relationships

He who appreciates another enriches himself far more than the one whom he praises. To praise is an investment in one's own happiness. The poorest human being has something to give that the richest could not buy.

—George Mathew Adams

*T*he neighbour who waves to you cheerfully and greets you with a bright smile and cheerful hello...

A friend who never fails to call you up and talk to you...

Your spouse who is always there for you...

Your mother who always has a piping hot meal ready for you when you return home...

Everyday we are witness to acts of loving kindness offered to us. Let us not dismiss them as small or trivial. They deserve to be appreciated.

It is our besetting fault that we often take people for granted. We eat what is placed on the table but fail to appreciate the person who cooked the meal. We lean on our friends for support, cry on their shoulders but fail to appreciate them for always *being there* for us.

Go up to people; reach out to praise them, thank them, appreciate them for what they have done and you will really make a difference!

Ludwig Von Beethoven was one of the greatest musicians the world has known. At the age of 11 he began to compose his music, and in his teens he won fame and fortune as a great composer.

One evening, Beethoven was passing by a cobbler's cottage, when he heard someone practising one of his compositions. As he paused to listen, he heard a girl exclaim, "I wish I could hear a real musician playing this piece, so that I could learn to render it properly!"

Beethoven entered the cottage and found a young girl seated at a piano. She was blind. Offering to play for her, he sat at the piano and played for an hour or so.

The girl was enthralled! Her appreciation fired the enthusiasm of Beethoven, and he went on playing. Dusk had set in; the cottage grew dark but the silvery moonlight filtered into the room. Under its inspiration and the whole-hearted warmth of the girl's appreciation, Beethoven composed his famous *Moonlight Sonata*.

Not all of us are blessed with great musical talent, or a captivating voice. Not all of us have what are called 'leadership qualities' or 'organising abilities'. We don't all win prizes, awards and scholarships. But all of us can and must cultivate the beautiful quality of appreciation. We must learn to praise others. It is no mean thing to possess this special talent for praising others, for without our appreciation, the brightest people in the world cannot shine!

Ask any famous singer: can he give a concert in an empty hall?

Ask a speaker: can he deliver an impassioned oration before his mirror?

Ask an actor: what would he be without his fans?

Ask a writer: whom is he writing for?

Appreciation works wonders. And don't think this is

confined to spiritual matters alone; it works in every field, every walk of life.

A distinguished Professor of the Kelloggs Business School, Deepak Jain, observes: "A leader will be truly successful only when his subordinates believe that they can grow under him."

How best can this impression be conveyed to them? Surely by the leader's words of appreciation and encouragement!

A young man who was about to begin his career was told by his father, "You must learn to give your best with or without appreciation. Don't let the quality of your work suffer because others do not praise you."

Sound words indeed. It is good *not to expect* appreciation for all that we do. But surely, nothing stops us from expressing appreciation for others! Now for example, if the young man's bosses had been told "Don't be content with just paying your workers' salary. Encourage them with your words of appreciation whenever possible!" What a world of difference it would have made to the young man's work!

Perhaps, husbands are more insensitive, more lacking in this aspect. A survey of women in rural America revealed that farmers' wives had one common complaint; they were taken for granted. They were hardly ever thanked for what they did.

One of them narrated an amusing incident. Everyday she took the trouble to make a delicious meal to set before her husband and sons when they returned home from work in the evening. She learnt new recipes. She prepared complicated dishes. It was obvious that they enjoyed the meal for it disappeared in no time at all. But not a word of thanks, not a single compliment was forthcoming.

In exasperation, she made a meal of cattle feed and set it, steaming hot, on the table one evening.

"What's this?" they screamed, when they had downed the first mouthful, "Are you crazy or what?"

"I have waited 26 years and not heard a word of praise from you," she replied. "I never ever thought that you would notice the difference."

Every now and then, all of us need to hear someone say to *us*, "I think you are wonderful!" And *we* need to say this to our friends, our colleagues and co-workers, our parents, spouses and children.

Why don't *you* utter these magic words of appreciation to someone today?

Dale Carnegie tells us, "Three-fourths of all the people you will ever meet are hungering and thirsting for appreciation. Give it to them and they will love you!" Indeed, appreciative words are the greatest incentive for doing good work.

When you tell your child, husband or friend that they are wrong, that they are insensitive or that they have done something badly, you take away their incentive for improvement. On the other hand, when you are liberal with your encouragement and appreciation, they will do their best and surprise you with what they can achieve!

Making others feel good about themselves builds better relationships. This is what Lord Chesterfield urges his son to do: Make every person like himself a little better, and he or she will begin to like you very much. Sincere praise reassures people. It dissolves the negative notions they have about themselves and improves their self-esteem.

Why Do We Complain?

**You can complain because roses have thorns, or you
can rejoice because thorns have roses.**

– Ziggy

$\mathcal{M}$any of us pass through certain phases of life,
'rough patches' as they are called, when
everything seems to go wrong for us. In such circumstances,
people do tend to become negative, and at such times, we
need to offer them help and support to carry them through,
and the inspiration and incentive to cultivate faith and
repose their trust in God.

But, there are some people who complain no matter
what happens to them! It seems that complaining has
become a way of life with them, that they simply cannot
stop cribbing! It seems to have nothing to do with
pessimism or optimism, pain or suffering: it just seems that
complaining has become second nature to them!

I must say that some of the people who suffer from pain
and illness, some of the patients I have met in hospitals are
not always of this type. They discover a lot to be grateful
for in the midst of their pain and affliction; they enjoy what
little respite they get from pain; they discover that such and
such movements of their limbs can be accomplished

without strain, and are very happy about it. They are happy to have visitors; they are grateful to the nursing staff; they thank their doctors for the relief they feel.

But some of us simply cannot stop complaining. Regardless of where they are, what they are doing, or what is happening to them, they keep on complaining! The traffic is too bad; the telephone lines are congested; the weather is too hot or too cold; people are rude or indifferent; servants are lazy and inefficient; the subordinates are insubordinate! And I could go on and on: nobody understands me; nobody appreciates me; nobody knows what I am going through; nobody cares; nobody helps; nobody knows...

Of course I feel sorry for such miserable people: but when I offer them a remedy for their misery, they refuse to take it! I say to them, "You try to be what others are not; you must try and appreciate others; you must care; you must understand; you must help others..."

They look at me as if I have suddenly switched over to Latin or Greek. They simply cannot register what I am saying to them. They want only to be at the receiving end of care, compassion, understanding, help, appreciation and sympathy. They do not want to give away any of those beautiful feelings to others!

Selfish people are born complainers. Nothing will ever convince them that a lot of people are far worse off than they are; nothing will persuade them that they have a lot to be grateful for; they prefer the martyr's syndrome: I am the most misunderstood, unappreciated creature in the entire world!

Complaints stem from a sense of unhappiness and dissatisfaction with life. But the way to meet this dissatisfaction is to set things right. Complaining constantly will only make things worse; and let us not forget – when we complain constantly, we become difficult and unpleasant to deal with and people would definitely like to keep their distance from us. Thus, we are cutting off the source of help and support that we feel we need so desperately!

All of us complain at one time or another: we are fed up with waiting interminably in a traffic jam or in a doctor's waiting room; we are angry when flight schedules are disrupted and our carefully laid travel plans are messed up completely; we react with indignation when government officers treat us with disrespect and callousness. This is but natural: in such situations, complaining, even loud complaining becomes a way of letting off steam, as we say. But the trouble starts when we make complaining a habit, and think that complaining is the best way to deal with life and its problems. Compulsive complainers make it their way of reacting to life. No matter what happens, they complain; they cry; they express their unhappiness volubly; they protest; they feel very sorry for themselves; they leave very little room for anyone else to step in and do anything for them!

People start complaining when they are unhappy; but complaining sometimes becomes a bad habit which they cannot get rid of. It is like those little children who get into the habit of sucking their thumb, and cannot thereafter give it up when they are scolded or pulled up. The worst thing is that many of them actually begin to feel better when they complain persistently: let me hasten to add, this is an entirely illusory feeling. They have managed to make the others miserable with their cribbing; they have unburdened themselves of all their negativity, and are entirely satisfied with their session: but the trouble is, their problems are no nearer to being solved.

People who complain constantly do not wish to take the responsibility for themselves and their actions. Ask them why their goals are not accomplished, and they will come up with excuses. What they don't realise is their energy and intellect is so focused on finding faults with others that they cannot concentrate on achieving their goals. They do not realise how tedious and futile their constant complaints are: they have effectively undermined their own power and efficiency, and have retained control only by constant complaining.

Constant complainers also suffer from a false sense of superiority because they are finding fault with everyone except themselves. They think others love listening to their complaints; they do not realise that they are actually driving away their friends, and will soon have only themselves left as their sole audience!

Just look at some of their complaints:

1. I am overworked and it is the fault of my boss. (What about your time management?)

2. I am late, and it is the fault of the public transport system. (Why don't you try leaving home early?)

3. My targets have not been met and it is the fault of my subordinates. (Why don't you lead from the front?)

4. My job is the most difficult and unpleasant. (Why don't you make way for someone who can handle it?)

5. I have been overlooked for promotion because the system is corrupt. (Have you looked at your own performance record?)

I said, all of us complain at one time or another. Dynamic complainers find a way to solve their problems; they give vent to their negativity through complaints and then go on to find a way out of their difficulties. Cribbers are far from dynamic; they are in fact defeatists who are more interested in making excuses and shifting the blame on to others. They are happy and satisfied just complaining: they do not want to lose control over their pet excuses.

Let's stop focusing on all that is wrong and focus instead on all that's right; let's stop cribbing about what we don't have and look instead at what's there for us; let's take the time to appreciate people for what they are and what they can do, instead of focusing on their defects. When we complain and criticise constantly, we are drawing negativities into our lives. Each time we utter something negative about life, we actually begin to believe it more and more, and make it come true in our lives. Our imagined ills become our reality. Needless to say, the reverse is also true. When we believe things are going good, they become better, actually. When we visualise success and talk about all that is positive, success actually begins to take shape for us.

So, let us stop complaining, start thanking, appreciating and feeling good about ourselves.

To this end, let me offer you a few practical suggestions.

Practical Suggestion 1:
Learn To Value People

> **Respect your fellow human beings, treat them fairly, disagree with them honestly, enjoy their friendship, explore your thoughts about one another candidly, work together for a common goal and help one another achieve it.**
>
> *—Bill Bradley*

*I*f you were to ask me to name one resource that we all undervalue, underrate and underutilise, I would say it is undoubtedly our Human Resource.

HR has now come to be a specialist term in Management; HR in former times was just people power; it wasn't just as 'staff' or 'resources' but as Mr. Joshi, Mrs. Khanna, Miss. Jones and Mrs. Krishnan that people were referred to. But then, as now, one thing stands true: if you don't value your people, you will lose them!

Recently, one of my friends who is an entrepreneur told me that a research project done in the US has found quantifiable proof that there is a direct correlation between how you treat the people who work for you and your company's financial results. People who are valued and appreciated give their best; and the best way to value people is to create an environment in which they are treated well and made to feel valued and appreciated.

Unfortunately, I know many 'bosses' and 'superiors' who do not like to convey their appreciation and value to their subordinates; they feel that these employees are doing what they are paid to do: why should we bother to appreciate them over and above the wages they are paid? The second reason is even more devious: praise someone, and chances are that he/she might expect a promotion or increment; might even get a 'big head'. So why inflate their ego? Get the work done and let them get on with the rest of the work.

Alas, people are stingy with praise. A manpower consultancy firm found that 58% of the employees they interviewed in a metro city, said that they did not even receive a simple thank-you note from their bosses for a job that was done well.

It was William James who said that the deepest need of a human being is the craving to be appreciated.

Praise helps people to reinstate their own self esteem. This, in turn, makes them enthusiastic about what they are doing; they find it worthwhile to achieve targets. Cash incentives, bonuses, perks and material benefits alone are not enough to retain people in an organisation and keep them motivated. We need to realise that people's sense of self worth and dignity are high value assets that need to be protected.

For those of us who are always worried about additional expenses, it is good to know that appreciation will make no dents in the pocket, and one can freely use it anytime, anywhere. In fact, a research carried out among young MBA students at a premier institution in India, found that the freshers valued appreciation more than a fat paycheck.

A successful business values its people as its assets, rather than as 'staff' or 'workforce'. A respected, well-treated employee is a satisfied employee who will work even harder to enhance his self-respect and prove his worth to an appreciative employer. It is not just a cliché to say "People are our number one assets". People are, in fact, the life-blood of an organisation.

Here is a list of simple and cost-effective techniques to boost morale among your employees:

- Learn to express your thanks in words, through official letters and notes
- Encourage people to come out with their suggestions and opinions. You may not agree with them; but it is good for you to know what they think
- Share a light moment with them; crack jokes, smile and laugh with them
- Remember to send them a note or a card on their birthdays
- Be sensitive to their needs
- Understand their perspective
- Encourage creativity and innovation through special awards
- Make sure that you have realistic expectations from people: remember, each one has different potential
- Do not try to exercise constant control over people and events. Just give them the right direction
- Praise deserving staff publicly and at meetings

Let me remind you, this applies not only to your employees, but also to your clients, suppliers and others.

An amusing story is told to us of Somerset Maugham, the famous author. His books had been published and sold in Spain, and Spanish laws did not permit him to take his enormous royalties out of the country at that time. Maugham decided that he would spend all the accumulated money in Spain, by taking a luxurious holiday at one of the famous Spanish resorts. He moved into a fine hotel, took their best suite, entertained his guests lavishly and had a great vacation. When he was fairly certain that most of the money had been spent, he asked for the bill, and announced at the Reception that he would be leaving the resort in a couple of days.

The Manager of the hotel called on him that afternoon. Maugham was told very politely that he had no bill to pay! His very presence at the hotel had been a matter of prestige to the proprietor; hundreds of visitors had been attracted to the hotel by Maugham's presence. The newspapers had written about his stay there. This had generated a lot of favourable publicity. There was no way that the hotel could charge a guest who had brought so much benefit to them!

The Spaniards knew how to value people!

Experts tell us of some distinct dimensions of managerial skills, which we do not normally associate with the conventional image of a 'boss'.

1) They are responsible, not only for the productivity, but for the happiness and emotional well-being of the people who work under them (Indirectly and directly, this affects productivity and profits too!).

2) Like the head of a family, or the coach of a sports team, the manager has an emotional responsibility towards his subordinates.

3) It is the manager and his style of functioning that makes the work environment stressful or comfortable; happy or strained; fun or hell.

4) While he has been hired by the organisation to promote its profits, the manager also has a more serious commitment to those who work under him – because their careers, their future are entrusted to his care.

5) It is not merely his job to tell people what to do: it is also his job to encourage people to contribute their ideas and suggestions on all projects undertaken by the company.

6) It is not enough for him to 'keep an eye' on the coming and going and doings of his people: it is also essential for him to give them the freedom and space where they will be able to function at their optimum level.

The best brains and the best talents in an organisation need to be nurtured in an environment that allows them to grow personally and professionally. A good manager keeps them focused, motivated and happy.

What kind of a manager are you?

What kind of a manager would you like to have as your boss?

Practical Suggestion 2:
Realise That No One Is Perfect

No one is perfect... that's why pencils have erasers.
—Author Unknown

*I*t was a wise man who said: "Only in grammar can you be more than perfect." And an Italian proverb warns us wryly: "He that will have a perfect brother must resign himself to remain brotherless."

And here is a brilliant piece of inductive reasoning: "I am a nobody. Nobody is perfect. Therefore, I am perfect."

The spirit of tolerance and acceptance is essential to a happy life and a peaceful mind. The world we live in is far from perfect; we are not ourselves paragons of perfection; and the same goes for the people around us. As they say, it's a crazy, mixed-up world – but we must recognise ourselves as part of all this imperfection, and accept life as it comes.

No One's Perfect is the best selling autobiography of Hirotada Ototake, who was born with a congenital condition that left him with almost no arms or legs. His parents determined that, as much as possible, he would live a 'normal' life. This means that he was given no special treatment neither at home nor at school, and ended up participating in schooling and sports. He went to the prestigious Wasada University – no mean achievement for anyone! *No One's Perfect* has become an instant best-seller in Japan. According to the publisher, it has sold over 4.5 million copies, the second largest selling book in the country in fifty years.

Until recently, people's tendency was to look at 'special' children as 'different' and somehow as distinct and separate from others: today, such an attitude is dismissed as prejudiced and incorrect and we are encouraged to appreciate them and applaud their efforts as we do with 'normal' children. They are treated like 'normal' children, as far as possible, and allowed to compete in sports and games amongst their own, sing, dance or paint, and receive due appreciation and prizes for their efforts – instead of being handed out a lot of 'sops' and sympathy. We are required to *understand* them and realise that they too, need to be treated like our fellow human beings who are differently abled, and not as if they belonged to a different species!

The greatest famine in the world today is the famine of understanding. No two people seem to understand each other today! Therefore, misunderstandings abound in our age. There is misunderstanding in our homes, our clubs, our schools, colleges, universities, corporations and organisations.

I recall the words of the great Parsi Prophet, Zoroaster: "Know well that a hundred temples of wood and stone have not the value of one understanding heart!"

Understanding hearts are what we need, so that people may live and work in harmonious, peaceful co-existence.

How and when can looking for perfection become problematic? Psychologists have the answer:

- Obsessive concern over others' mistakes
- Setting excessively high standards for ourselves and others around us
- Unreasonable doubts about others' ability to perform tasks
- An over-emphasis on 'control' and 'benchmarks'

Striving for perfection, while accepting that perfection rarely can be achieved, can lead to growth and development and a feeling of satisfaction. It can be a powerful motivator as long as it is based on reasonable standards and expectations.

Thus far, I have been saying that we must understand that no one is perfect: let me add a note of request now; this does not mean that we must stop striving for perfection! And no, I am not contradicting myself! We must constantly strive for perfection. To most of us, this striving for perfection will be a lifelong journey, for as someone has said, perfection is always a moving target. Let us strive for perfection so that we may know how difficult it is to achieve; and, in this process of striving, let us come to understand, condone and accept imperfection in our fellow human beings, especially those who are in a subordinate position to us.

"Be ye therefore perfect, even as your Father in heaven is perfect," Jesus tells us in the Bible. May we not conclude that he urges us to imitate God, and therefore be loving, kind and forgiving to everyone around us, irrespective of how smart and clever and useful they are to us. Let us instead be filled with the spirit of compassion and mercy, that enables us to accept others as they are, instead of expecting perfection from them.

Sri Krishna too, in the Gita refers to perfection: "It is better to perform one's own duties imperfectly than to master the duties of another. By fulfilling the obligations he is born with, a person never comes to grief."

In case you are wondering which duty he refers to, let me give you the words of a Krishna devotee who sums up the teaching of the Gita for us: "Be fearless and pure; never waiver in your determination or your dedication to the spiritual life. Give freely. Be self-controlled, sincere, truthful, loving, and full of the desire to serve. Learn to be detached and to take joy in renunciation. Do not get angry or harm any living creature, but be compassionate and gentle; show good will to all. Cultivate vigour, patience, will, purity; avoid malice and pride. Then, you will achieve your destiny."

What does it mean to be compassionate and gentle, kind and loving and patient? It is surely to accept people with their imperfections and weaknesses, and still continue to appreciate their worth. If they are imperfect, why, so are we!

Practical Suggestion 3:
Look For Merits – Not Defects

If the sight of the blue skies fills you with joy, if the simple things of nature have a message that you understand, rejoice for your soul is alive.

–Eleonora Duse

*W*e cannot have 'theories' for everything – especially for getting along with people. No blueprint can give us a preplanned design to organise our lives with other people. Human beings are unique, perhaps somewhat illogical, and definitely unprogrammable! Each one of us is sensitive; each one of us is different; and each one of us is constantly variable – our mood and temperament change from day to day, may be even from hour to hour!

And yet we have evolved into a society, into a community, into a global habitat with families, institutions and corporations. This has been possible with time, a growing sense of awareness, and a great deal of understanding, tolerance, sympathy and mutual respect. Every relationship is unique and special. Parents, spouses, children, family, friends, neighbours, colleagues, superiors, subordinates, employers or employees – every relationship needs to be nurtured with understanding and patience.

The secret of successful relationships is found in an understanding heart – preferably, your own! The secret of a harmonious and peaceful life is: Focus on people's merits and strengths – not on their weaknesses and defects.

The great Prophet of the Baha'i faith, Baha'ullah, said to his disciples again and again, "If you find that there are nine vices and only one virtue in your neighbour, forget the nine vices, and focus only on the one virtue." This is the secret of an understanding heart. See only the good in others. When we focus on others' faults, we only draw those negative forces unto ourselves. Fault-finding, constant criticism and magnifying the mistakes of others are poor, ineffective ways of changing the world. A sunny temperament and a healthy sense of humour can do wonders for you. Learn to laugh with others; try a smile or a kind word – you will find that wrongs are easy to set right, and 'wrong doers' are set back on the right track!

When we constantly criticise others and find fault with them, we hurt them with tongue-lashes, which, in some cases, are worse than whip-lashes! An ancient poet tells us that the tongue is a very powerful instrument. It should be used largely for uttering the name of the Lord. Instead, if we use the tongue only to find fault with others, we are abusing the God-given power of speech and language. The poet adds that there are four grievous wrongs that our tongues can commit: (1) Uttering falsehood (2) Scandal mongering/ gossipping (3) Finding fault with others and (4) Excessive talk.

Ella Wheeler Wilcox tells us pretty much the same thing:
> Give words of comfort, of defence and hope,
> To mortals crushed by sorrow and by error.
> And though thy feet through shadowy paths may grope,
> Thou shalt not walk in loneliness or terror.

Of a great English poet, I read that he never spoke a word of appreciation to his wife. So long as she lived he criticised her and found fault with everything that she did. Suddenly, the wife died. The poet was grief-stricken. He was ashamed that he had failed to write poems in appreciation of her, when she had been alive. "If only I had known," he lamented. "If only I had known..."

Truly it has been said, life is too short to be small. Let us not be small-minded. Let us be generous with praise, appreciation and encouragement.

The great artist of the Renaissance, Leonardo da Vinci said: "Never reprove a friend in public. Always praise him in front of others."

Some of us insist on pointing a finger at others' shortcomings. "Someone's got to change all that is wrong with this world," we proclaim. Let me tell you, fault-finding and magnifying others' mistakes are poor ways of changing the world.

When I find fault with others, I regard myself as superior– better than the others. This is pride, this is egoism. This must be overcome if we are to be truly happy.

There is a beautiful incident narrated to us by the great Sufi poet Sadi. When Sadi was a young boy of six, his father, a *dervish*, took him to the mosque where a night-long vigil was being observed. As the night grew, Sadi found that one after another, the people who had assembled at the mosque began to fall asleep. Even the *mullah* had nodded off. Only Sadi and his father had remained awake.

The little boy whispered into the ears of his father, "Father, only you and I are keeping the vigil. All the others have fallen asleep."

Sadi's father admonished him, "It is better to go off to sleep and not observe the vigil, rather than find fault with others and think ourselves superior."

If you wish to be happy, you can begin by thinking, "Everybody has something good in him; there is something that I can learn from every human being."

Tina was a 'special' child – severely challenged physically and intellectually. Her parents brought her to experts who would observe her carefully, access her capabilities and suggest a child-centred approach which her parents could adopt to teach her at home. The experts would not impose any set programmes on Tina; rather they would learn her preferences and inclinations first, and allow the child to guide them in helping her. During successive sessions, trained volunteers and special teachers would observe the child, and share their observations with each other and the parents.

At the end of the third day's session, Neela, one of the volunteers said enthusiastically, "Yesterday, Tina was not ready to move out of her place; but this morning, when I held out a toy to her, she actually took a few steps in my direction."

Shanti, another volunteer added, "This afternoon, when I showed her a teddy bear, she laughed happily and came to me to touch the teddy."

Tina's mother, who was listening open-mouthed, interjected at this point, "But...but she *cannot* walk!"

"Oh?" said the volunteers politely, "We really didn't know that!"

I narrated this real-life story that I read recently to tell you how the teachers and trainers of 'special' children do not pre-judge the capabilities of their young wards. This is an attitude we will all do well to adopt.

We have ingrained notions of what is right and wrong, what is proper and improper, what is acceptable and unacceptable. When we impose our narrow and harsh judgements on others, we condemn ourselves to a critical attitude and lose out on a lot of good cheer and joy that comes from being open-minded.

As I said to you earlier, none of us is perfect. No man or woman can ever be perfect. Even Jesus said to us, "Call me not perfect. Alone the Father in heaven is perfect!" Marriage, friendship, any relationship or business partnership involves two imperfect human beings trying to live together, work together or establish a link. Unless we learn to accept people as they are, we will lose all possibility of finding happiness in our relationships.

A stranger arrived at the gates of a city, which he was visiting for the first time. An old woman sitting on the roadside greeted him, "Welcome to our city."

"What kind of people live here?" the stranger asked her.

"What kind of people live in your home town?" the old woman asked him with a smile.

"Oh, they were terrible," swore the stranger. "They were mean, nasty, malicious and selfish. They were impossible to live with."

"You will find people here are pretty much the same," the old woman said to him.

A little later, another stranger arrived at the city gates, and was welcomed by the old woman.

"What kind of people live in this city?" the second traveller asked.

"How did you find them in your home town?" the woman asked him.

"They were a wonderful lot – hard working, friendly, and easy to get along with."

"You will find the people here likewise," the old woman assured him.

Approach people with love and understanding – and you will find the same reflected in their approach to you.

I read a story about an angel who shrank and dwindled when spoken to harshly, but expanded to its full stature and shone with radiance when spoken to kindly and treated lovingly.

See the good in others! Utter kind words and loving thoughts about them. You will find that this has a healing effect on them and you. Harsh words and criticism cause people to shrink and wither. The happy, positive individual does not criticise, he does not find fault with others. If we too begin to see the good in others we will keep on growing better and better and our minds will always be at peace, and the world around us will smile.

Practical Suggestion 4:
Take The Lead In

We can only be said to be alive in those moments when our hearts are conscious of our treasures.

—Thornton Wilder

*H*uman relationships thrive on caring, sharing and mutual appreciation. We rely on our loved ones, our friends and those closest to us, for moral support and encouragement.

No one knows who wrote or said these lines originally, but all of us have read these lines and been inspired by them:

> I shall pass through this world but once. Any good, therefore, that I can do, or any kindness that I can show to any human being, let me do it now. Let me not defer nor neglect it, for I shall not pass this way again.

The popular writer Dale Carnegie calls this one of the basic requirements for happiness in life. "Cut out this quotation and put it where you will see it every morning!" he tells us.

Is it not true that all of us feel happy when we are appreciated? In this, as in other things, what we send out comes back to us. For life is like a boomerang: what we are, what we do, comes back to us. When we give our best to the world, when we send out warmth, love and appreciation – it all comes back to us.

There are very many occasions in life which call for celebration – special events like a birth or a wedding in the family, birthdays, promotions, a new home, etc. But, let us not forget that each and every day is filled with numerous things which deserve our appreciation and gratitude. If only we would pause, reflect and consider life's countless blessings, we would realise how much there is to be appreciated in life!

Appreciate nature! The blue sky above you, the green grass at your feet, the magnificent hills, the vast seas, life-giving, life-generating rivers and the beauty and grandeur of gardens and woods.

Appreciate each day that comes to you out of the spotless hands of God. Think of all that you take for granted – your life that is a great gift, your good health, which is a blessing, your family which is precious, and the joy and love that come to you from all around. Learn to appreciate all the beauty and warmth which we so often ignore!

Above all, appreciate people! Human relationships need to be nurtured. We often think of our friends, spouses and parents as 'pillars of strength' which are always there for our solid support. I urge you, occasionally think of them as precious plants that need constant tending!

When tensions are rising and troubles are mounting, it is people who are close to us that bear the brunt of our stress. We are often courteous, polite and kind to perfect strangers, but rude and brusque to our own spouses and parents.

Many relationships suffer from sheer neglect and

indifference. It was a wise man – perhaps, it was a wise woman – who said, "Even love has a shelf life".

A Rabbi was offering special counselling sessions to his congregation on nurturing marital relationships. An old man went up to the Rabbi and offered his help. "I know the secret of marital bliss," he asserted vigorously. "It's very simple."

"I'm the expert on the subject," the old man said, gleefully. "I ought to know, because I've been married four times."

The Rabbi was taken aback, and his shock must have shown on his face. The old man laughed at the expression on his face and added, "To the same woman."

He proceeded to explain that he and his wife had been married for 45 years. The first marriage was when he and his wife had been young and carefree. The second was when they had been rearing their three children. The third was when the children grew up and left home. The fourth was when they both retired.

"Each of these marriages called for different ground rules," the old man said. "We gave each other the love and appreciation and support we needed as the situation and circumstances of our life changed. We married each other – over and over again!"

There is nothing like warmth, love and appreciation to revitalise relationships!

If only we look around us, if only we see and listen with care, we will never complain that life is boring and dull! When you learn to appreciate the world and its people you will find the grass greener; you will see that the moon shines brighter; and the dreariness of life will disappear, leaving fresh colours and fragrances behind!

John Ruskin, the distinguished Victorian writer remarked, "I am not surprised at what men suffer from, but I am surprised at what men miss out on!"

"Take time to live – because the world has so much to give!" proclaimed the caption of a beautiful picture which I saw in a friend's house. All of us need to take time to live – to appreciate all the good things and wonderful people around us. This is sure to bring us, and them, a great deal of happiness.

There is a world of beauty and charm lying out there for us – and, we are blind to it. We lack the quality of appreciation. Therefore, let us take the lead in appreciation.

Practical Suggestion 5:
We Need One Another!

No one can whistle a symphony. It takes a whole orchestra to play it.

—H. E. Luccock

*R*ecently I met an industrialist who had bagged a major export order for his company. I congratulated him and remarked that his people had indeed done him proud. His whole demeanour changed from one of self-satisfaction to mild vexation. "My people?" he said sarcastically. "Believe me, those people have done nothing for me or my company," he snarled. "Whatever I have achieved, it is despite their inefficiency and non-cooperation. I am working to cover up their ineptitude and serious lapses. My chief accountant is not to be trusted. My marketing team has to be monitored constantly. As for my workers, the less said about them, the better."

I thought to myself, that if his workforce was indeed as bad as he put it, he would probably have had to close down his operations! The truth was, he would have been happy to shift the blame on to them if that had happened. But now, he was doing rather well; and he did not want to share the credit with them.

I am afraid many of us are guilty of this attitude. We fail to give credit where it is due; we are reluctant to acknowledge the role that others have played in our success; we feel that we alone are responsible for our achievements.

What can anyone achieve on his own? How can we ignore the idea of our mutual interdependence? In the powerful words of John Donne, "No man is an island, entire of itself...".

The well known American singer and social activist, Joan Baez, used Donne's idea to create one of her best known songs:

> No man is an island,
> No man stands alone,
> Each man's joy is joy to me,
> Each man's grief is my own.
> We need one another,
> So I will defend,
> Each man as my brother,
> Each man as my friend.

Mahatma Gandhi observes that one of the basic truths about human beings is that they are necessarily interdependent, and together, form an organic whole. This interdependence begins at the time of our birth – for we would never live to become teenagers or adults without the sacrifices made by our parents, guardians and caretakers. We achieve our true potential in a peaceful, stable and secure society which allows us to flourish at our best. The contribution of thousands upon thousands of anonymous men and women makes our everyday life smooth and trouble-free. If we achieve a measure of greatness or success as intellectuals, we owe a debt of gratitude to the countless saints and sages and men of genius who have shown us the way. We benefit too, from a rich world of God's creation to which we ourselves have contributed nothing. In short, as Gandhiji concludes, every human being owes his humanity to others. Thus, according to Gandhiji, we are all 'born debtors', for whom a lifetime is not enough to pay back what we owe to our parents as well as thousands of benefactors who have contributed directly or indirectly to all that we are and all that we have achieved.

Have you ever stopped to think what a great debt of gratitude you owe to others?

How can we ever begin to repay these debts? Only by acknowledging the contributions that others have made for our benefit, and by doing what little we can for others, in our own way. The farmer grows the food that is put on my table; the tradesmen deliver the groceries and articles that make my daily routine smooth. What can I do for them? I may not be able to go and help the farmer in his field or the grocer in his shop; but I can pay my taxes honestly; I can deal with all tradesmen kindly and generously; I can do my bit to make this world better in some way or the other. If all else is impossible for me, I can at least spread a little sunshine with my smile and good cheer!

It is no surprise therefore, that Gandhi felt that the whites in South Africa were not just ill-treating the blacks, but actually degrading and brutalising them by their cruel behaviour. The wrongs they committed against humanity were injurious to their own dignity as human beings.

It is not right for us to say with Cain, "I am not my brother's keeper". We all have heard of that terrible story in the Book of Genesis, where the man who murders his brother shirks his moral responsibility, and utters these words to God. His words have now come to symbolise people's unwillingness to accept responsibility for the welfare and well-being of their fellow human beings. But, if truth be told, we are indeed our brothers' keepers; and our brothers are our keepers. Where would we be without one another? And, what is more germane to our theme, how can we fail to be grateful for all that others have done, are doing and will continue to do for us?

There are situations in life when we come to realise that our money and social position are of very little use to us. We have to accept our own limitations, and look to our fellow human beings for help and support. Think of a medical emergency when you or your loved ones have to be hospitalised. Think of a railway accident when the passengers have to rely on the rescue efforts of hundreds of volunteers. Think of visiting an unknown city or a foreign country where you know no one at all. In such situations, we get by only with the help of an orderly public administration system, a well regulated police force and friendly people who are ready and willing to help perfect strangers like us and make us feel at home! We gain from others when we realise that as human beings, we are all inter-dependent. We learn from others when we realise that we need their help, and seek the same with humility. At such times, we come to realise how little we know, and how we cannot get on without others. However, we would miss these valuable insights, if our pride and ego stand in our way. There is so much wisdom to be learned from the people around us. Life offers so many opportunities for us to evolve emotionally and intellectually. And the most valuable lessons in life are learned when we accept that other people have contributed something indispensable to our lives, and also begin to appreciate their share in our well being. Some of us are blessed with material wealth and riches; some of us are blessed with business acumen; some are gifted with artistic bent and creativity; yet others stand apart with their caring and compassionate attitude; a few of us are efficient and capable administrators; sincerity and devotion mark the efforts of some people; the world needs us all. We can each contribute our own special and unique efforts to make life more meaningful and beautiful. What matters is that we recognise the others' contributions and appreciate them. All of us, with our individual gifts and skills are like so many strings on God's lute. We will make divine music when we function together.

Many of us feel lost in the immensity of life. Many of us feel unwanted or insignificant in the workplace. Things seem to happen with or without our contribution. Major events and functions happen where we do not have a role to play. At best we are reduced to the level of bystanders or spectators; at worst, we feel unwanted, useless, redundant. This naturally causes a great deal of unhappiness in our hearts. Appreciate others! Make everyone feel they are important and that their welfare and happiness matter to you personally.

A group of executives and administrators were having dinner at the restaurant. They talked about the various problems that beset religion, and the talk turned to Christianity. "If you ask me, Jesus should have considered his choice of followers a little more critically," one of them said. "He should have looked among rulers and leaders, or at skilled statesmen and gifted orators. Instead, what did he do? He went to the shores of Lake Galilee and called out four common fishermen – Peter, Andrew, James and John. I can't help thinking he might have chosen better," the man continued. "He might have chosen more educated, more cultured, more appropriate people, don't you agree?"

"I don't agree with you," said a diner who sat at the next table. "Excuse me, but I could not help overhearing your conversation. And I would like to say this on behalf of the fishermen – they too have very many positive, strong points. They are resourceful, patient and persevering. They have the courage to weather many storms. They know how to take care of their boats, tackle and equipment. They know what it is to brave the elements and struggle against harsh conditions. They know how to work as a team and care for each other." God chooses His own people for each task. To us, they might seem unlikely choices – but He knows they are right for His plan. 'They' might be you and me – for we too, have our own role to play in God's scheme of things. All we need to do is to remember that in this vast and panoramic drama of life, our roles would be meaningless if it were not for the parts played by others.

Practical Suggestion 6:
Give People What They
Deserve And A Little More!

There is no happiness in having or in getting, but only in giving.

–Henry Drummond

*I*n Shakespeare's play *Hamlet*, the prince welcomes a group of wandering actors who have come to the palace and requests the minister at the court to attend to their hospitality. The minister replies rather stiffly and pompously that they will be treated 'according to their deserts', i.e. as they deserve. What he means is that they are just poor actors, far beneath him on the social scale, and they can be treated like inferiors. The prince responds swiftly, in words that are like a whiplash on our conscience, "If we were to treat every man according to 'his deserts' none of us shall escape whipping!"

"Use them after your own honor and dignity the less they deserve, the more merit is in your bounty," the prince adds.

Let us treat people as we would like to be treated by them. Who are we to judge another's worth? What if God were to apply the same scales to us as we apply to others? In this aspect, let us err on the side of generosity, compassion and kindness, so that God may look at us with mercy rather than justice.

Students at a Management Institute were made to answer a quiz at the end of the first year of their course. Many of them answered nine out of the ten questions pretty quickly, but were taken aback by the tenth question:

What is the first name of the lady who cleans the Institute every morning?

On the way out of the class, one of them asked the professor, if the last question would be counted in their quiz grade.

"But of course," he answered. "Why do you ask?"

"Well..." she stammered, "I was just wondering what the servant's name had to do with the test..."

The professor smiled and said to her, "In your careers, you will meet many people. All of them will be significant. They will deserve your attention and care, even if all you do is smile and say 'Hello'. This question was to prepare you for that attitude!"

In the days when an ice cream sundae cost very little, a ten-year-old boy entered the restaurant in a busy shopping centre and sat at a table. A waitress put a glass of water in front of him.

"How much is an ice cream sundae?" he asked hesitantly.

"Fifty cents," replied the waitress.

The little boy pulled his hand out of his pocket and counted the coins painstakingly. Then he looked up at the waitress and asked in a small voice, "Well, how much is a plain dish of ice cream?"

By now, people were beginning to arrive and there were a few who were waiting for a table. The waitress was growing impatient. "Thirty-five cents," she replied brusquely, and added for good measure in a stern voice, "make up your mind, sonny".

The little boy again counted his coins. "I'll have the plain ice cream, please," he said. The waitress brought the ice cream, put the bill on the table and walked away. The boy finished the ice cream, put his money on the bill and left.

When the waitress came back, she began to cry as she wiped down the table. There, placed neatly beside the empty dish, were fifty cents! The boy could actually have had the sundae that he longed for; but he had chosen to have plain ice cream rather than leaving the waitress without a tip!

A CEO of a Fortune 500 company tells us: "How you treat other CEOs is not as important to me, as how you treat waiters in restaurants and cleaners and assistants in the office."

The man who first came up with the waiter-theory, or at least first wrote it down, is the CEO of Raytheon Company, called Bill Swanson. He wrote a booklet of 33 short leadership observations and called it *Swanson's Unwritten Rules of Management*. Raytheon has given away 250,000 of the books.

Among those 33 rules is one that Swanson says never fails: "A person who is nice to you but rude to the waiter, or to others, is not a nice person."

"Watch out for people who have a situational value system, who can turn the charm on and off depending on the status of the person they are interacting with," Swanson writes. "Be especially wary of those who are rude to people perceived to be in subordinate roles."

"Treat people as if they were what they ought to be, and you help them to become what they are capable of being," writes the great German author, Goethe.

Do you treat people well because they are good looking, wear expensive clothes and jewels or arrive in an expensive car? You are not exhibiting a desirable personality trait!

Give others the best treatment that you are capable of: it may not say much about them, but it reveals the truth about you.

Do not judge others harshly, lest God should do the same to you!

Practical Suggestion 7:
Offer Thanks To God Every
Moment Of Your Life!

> Gratefulness is the key to a happy life that we hold in our hands, because if we are not grateful, then no matter how much we have we will not be happy—because we will always want to have something else or something more.
>
> *—Brother David Steindl-Rast*

*T*oday, scientists are beginning to understand the value and power of thought energy. They are beginning to study what our ancient *rishis* knew thousands of years ago. I am indeed happy that this truth has been reaffirmed in our days by influential thinkers and scientists. One of the fundamental laws of life is that, 'Energy follows thought'. Hence whatever we think, it somehow happens. If we fear a fall, we fall down. To put it simply, we are what we think. Hence we should be very careful with our thoughts.

Thoughts have an inherent capacity to materialise.

Life gives us a choice between Positivism and Negativism. If you want to be a winner in life, then choose to be positive. A positive person is happy under all circumstances. His life has a 'subtle' energy which keeps him happy and contended.

A positive man, a man of contentment, is known by his attitude to the things happening around him. In every situation, under all conditions he says, "Praised be the

Lord! Whatever He does, whatever He gives me, is worthy of praise." This attitude of acceptance with gratitude is the secret of true contentment. But it should be genuine. It should come from the depths of your heart; only then would you experience the freedom you seek.

A man of contentment will praise the Lord and express his gratitude even when he is passing through stormy weather or facing the worst crisis of life. A man of contentment is always at peace with himself and the world. He does not lose his temper nor does he complain or blame others for his condition, because he knows that whatever God does has a meaning and purpose for him. And so he believes, " *Tum Hi Sabh Kuch Jaanat Pritam Tere Ichha Puran Ho, Dukh Mein, Sukh Mein Mere Pritam Tere Ichha Puran Ho* – You know everything my Beloved, Let Thy will always be done. In joy and sorrow my Beloved, Let Thy will always be done. "

Let me be the first to warn you, this is rather difficult to practise. There is always a conflict between 'my' will and God's Will. I may want to go in one direction, but God may pull me and show me another direction. This not only causes conflict but it causes frustration. Hence, to avoid this state of frustration we should learn to cultivate the spirit of detachment, and accept the Will of God. By accepting God's Will in a spirit of detachment, we will escape from the vicious cycle of desire-disappointment-frustration-pain, and acquire the spirit of contentment. We will begin to experience the peace that passeth, indeed surpasseth understanding.

May I pass on to you a *mantra* which is sure to bring you peace, contentment and serenity? It is an expression of your utter and complete faith in the Almighty. It is a prayer which a saint, a holy man of God used to offer again and again. Inscribe it on the tablet of your heart. Repeat it again and again—remember it by day and night, for it is really simple:

Yes Father, Yes Father—Yes and always Yes!

Yes Father, Yes Father—Yes and always Yes!

There are people who are upset with me because I advocate the philosophy of grateful acceptance. They say to me, that this will make people lazy and lethargic; they will give up all their drive and ambition and simply sink into passive resignation.

I beg to differ with them on this point. I do not think people will become lazy and lethargic if they follow the philosophy of acceptance. I believe true acceptance in the right spirit is a dynamic concept which encourages us to do our very best, to put forth our best efforts to achieve what we desire. But if we cannot achieve those results, you must accept it as the Will of God, in the knowledge that there must be some good in it. As I always say, there is a meaning of mercy in all the incidents and accidents of life. Therefore let us accept everything with the *mantra*, "Yes Father, yes, and always, yes!"

There is a meaning of mercy in all that happens to us, for God is all love and all wisdom. He is too loving to punish us. He is too wise to make a mistake. Therefore if something comes to me that is contrary to my personal will, I must accept it as the Will of God. As Gurudev Sadhu

Vaswani taught us, "Every disappointment is His appointment."

Acceptance with due gratitude is also a subtle law, which puts you on the path of self-growth. "O God, whatever You do and whatever happens has a purpose and a meaning. Your scheme of things is perfect. I accept your Will." This should be your attitude in life; and whether you succeed or fail, ever remain grateful to God.

Sadhu Vaswani in his sacred verses has said,

> Thank You, Thank You, O Lord,
> Grateful to You,
> Wherever I am.
> Whatever I am.
> *Shukkur*. I accept it all.

Every accomplishment, every form of excellence, every success, small or big, belongs to God. If you are wise and intelligent, it is God-given. If your hard work and effort are commendable, it is due to the grace of God. If you are truly conscious of this, and acknowledge His grace in all humility – why, this humility too is a manifestation of His mercy upon you.

Whenever there are hurdles in life or problems beyond your control, seek God's help. To cross the hurdles, to solve the problems and to meet the challenges of life, you need inner strength. You can get this strength by appealing to the Supreme *Shakti*, the All-Powerful, the Almighty. Seek His strength. Appeal to Him: O Supreme *Shakti*, give me strength. "Would you know who is the greatest saint in the world?" asks William Law. "It is not he who prays most or fasts most; it is not he who gives most alms or is most eminent for temperance, charity or justice; but it is he who is always thankful to God; who wills everything God wills, who receives everything as an instance of God's Goodness and has a heart always ready to praise God for it."

Make this the *mantra* of your life: "Yes Father, yes, and always yes!"

A lady on a long haul transcontinental flight was terrified when the jet hit strong turbulence. Nervously, she asked the flight stewardess, "Are we going to crash?"

"Of course not," the stewardess smiled. "Don't worry. We are all safe in God's hands."

The woman's eyes widened with shock. "Oh my!" she exclaimed, "Is it that bad?"

"No!" said the stewardess emphatically. "It's that good!"

As ordinary mortals, we have so many imperfections, defects, errors, weaknesses and insufficiencies. We are often overcome by doubt and insecurities. It becomes essential that we all learn to put ourselves in God's hands and allow ourselves to be guided by His Divine Wisdom.

Acceptance in the spirit of gratitude unlocks the fullness in our lives. It can turn despair into faith, strife into harmony, chaos into order, and confusion into clear understanding. It restores peace into our hearts and helps us to look forward to the morrow in the faith that God is always with us!

It is not enough to speak of gratitude or enact deeds of gratitude – we must live gratitude by practising acceptance of God's Will in all conditions, in all incidents and accidents of life.

Wisdom consists in accepting God's Will – not with despair or resignation, but in peace and faith, in absolute gratitude, knowing that our journey through life has been perfectly planned by Infinite love and Infinite wisdom. There can be no mistake in God's plan for us!

Again and again, we try to run away from difficult situations; again and again we rebel, react with anger and bitterness. How can we ever be at peace?

The answer is simple: Grow in the spirit of gratitude to God; develop the spirit of acceptance. "Not my will, but Thy will be done, O Lord!" This must be the constant utterance on your lips.

You should always remember, that God is with you. Tell yourself constantly: He is my Father and Mother. He is the One who protects all of us at all times. We have to have a direct hotline with God! We should talk to Him; have a dialogue with Him and sure enough He will show us the way. Build up faith in Him. Believe in Him.

If all else fails you, remember the Lord's promise to us in the Gita: Renouncing all rites and writ duties, come unto me for single refuge – seek refuge at His Holy Feet. He will never ever let you down!

Positive thinking, like gratitude, is not instantaneous. To be positive, to cultivate the spirit of thanksgiving, you have to put in effort. I am often told by a few friends, that in spite of much effort, some of them are unable to get rid of grudges, complaints and negativism. Maybe in some rare cases, one life is not sufficient to take away the negativism of numerous previous births. But you must continue your efforts ceaselessly, and some day out of the blue you will see, the clouds disperse and the sun shines brightly!

PRACTICAL EXERCISES IN
THANKSGIVING
FOR EVERY DAY OF THE MONTH

Choose any of these suggestions at random,
and put them into practise at least for a day.
Feel the difference that it makes to you and to
others whose lives you touch.

1. Who are the people to whom you owe an infinite debt of gratitude?

Our parents gave us the gift of this human birth. They took care of us when we were utterly helpless. They stood by us when we needed them.

Let us bow down to them with deep reverence of the heart and in some form of the other express our gratitude

2. Several failures and disappointments have helped us to shape our life. Think of five of them and express gratitude to God!

3. All around you are the beauties of nature. Today, let us thank each and every aspect of Nature. In silence, offer your thanks to each and every little thing that makes this earth the beautiful planet that it is, for us to enjoy! Think of the green grass, the trees, the birds in the sky, the clouds, the stars and the moon, the breeze, the rain... Imagine what life on earth would be like without them! Give gratitude to God for having given you the gift of sight and pray for atleast one blind man who is denied this great privilege

4. Today we shall make an earnest effort to appreciate those that do not understand us and criticise us at every step, in every round of life. We shall count our blessings and feel grateful for everyone of them! Where would we be without them?

5. Take time to live – because life has so much to give! Today, take time to appreciate all the things and people who make your life worth living

6. Today, let us give gratitude to those whom the world regards as fellow *shevakas* – but without whose help and active service the world would not be a clean place to live in – for eg. domestic servants, the laundryman and the street sweepers. Let us thank them and offer them some little token of our appreciation

7. Today, let us express our gratitude to those whom we take for granted but without whom life would become an unbearable burden – for eg. family members and friends

8. Today, let us give gratitude to God, who has provided us with the five senses – sight, smell, taste, touch and hearing without which we would be no better than stones

9. Today, let us give gratitude to God for the gift of a healthy body without which life would become an unbearable burden for ourselves and others around us

10. Today, let us offer our gratitude for all those people who are always negative in their attitude and outlook. Thank you God for having given us the wisdom and the strength to respond in a positive way to everything that happens to us

11. Today, let us begin the day by offering the simple prayer, "Thank you God for everything". Let this prayer be on our lips throughout the day. If we get a free minute let us utilise it in repeating this prayer, "Thank you God for everything"

12. Begin the day by sitting in a silent corner and take in deep breaths. With every incoming breath, breathe out an aspiration: I feel grateful for the many blessings that I have received. With every outgoing breath, say: these blessings are not for me alone. I must share them with those in need

13. Think of all the great ones who have influenced your life one way or the other. Feel grateful that such great ones always keep on coming to the earth plane for our sake

....
....
....
....
....
....
....
....
....
....
....
....
....
....
....
....
....
....
....
....
....
....
....
....
....
....
....
....
....
....
....
....
....

14. Today make a list of emotional strengths you have that help you cope with the challenges of life: Are you reliable? Are you trustworthy? Are you punctual? Are you friendly? Are you responsible? Are you understanding? Thank God for these positive traits. Appreciate yourself as a person with these beautiful virtues

15. Today dedicate your gratitude to the teachers who have helped to mould you, make you, shape you and bring out your special strengths. If you can, get in touch with atleast one of them and express your love and respect to him / her

16. Thank you God for forgiving all my faults and failings and giving me a chance to live the new life – a life of simplicity and service, of purity and prayer

17. What would life be without comforts? Make a list of all the comforts that you enjoy. From a cozy home, music, a vehicle, our gadgets, even a clean toilet at the workplace. Count these blessings one by one and send out your gratitude to God for them

18. Each one of us is blessed with talents. Make a list of the talents you possess and feel grateful for them. You may be a good singer, a painter, a dancer, or just a good conversationist. Feel blessed and thank God for these talents

19. What would life be like without friends with whom we can share our joys and sorrows? Without being judgmental, love them and thank them for their friendship and support. Make a list today of the great friends who have made your life a happy journey! Call up at least one of them to express your appreciation and to tell them what a difference they have made to your life

20. Think of all the different types of foods (vegetarian) that have been provided on earth for man to eat and give thanks especially for those types which you like the most

21. Do music and songs make you forget your worries and woes? Give thanks to the masters of music without whom our life would be dry as the desert sands

22. Every person has some faults and failings, weaknesses and imperfections. Prepare a list of your faults and surrender it to the Lord with a prayer: "I can't do it Lord. But, You in Your mercy can free me from these faults. Thank You God! Thank You God!"

23. Think of problems as steps of the ladder that lead to the Highest and pray, "In Thy mercy Thou hast sent me these problems. Grant me the wisdom and the strength to solve them and draw nearer and ever more near to Thee!"

24. Thank God for laughter and smiles, good humour and merriment! Laugh out loud as often as you can today. Share a joke or two with your colleagues. Spread the sunshine of laughter around you

25. Make today a no-cribbing day. Just for today, give up criticising, complaining, and finding fault with others. Take life as it comes; take people as they are; do not sit in judgement upon anything or anyone, just for today

26. Make today a gratitude-to-God day. Thank God for every incident – good or bad that happens to you today

27. Make today an Appreciation Day. Appreciate every person you meet and try to express that appreciation in words. This includes your near and dear ones – your spouse and siblings – your children and friends, your fellow colleagues and your servants

28. Today you must make every person, who meets you, feel that he is a very important person

29. Today let the words, "May I help you" be on your lips all the time

30. Today let me visit a sick friend or carry fruits and distribute them to the poor patients in the government hospital

31. Are you one of those blessed souls fortunate enough to have the grace of a Guru's presence in your life? Today, thank your Guru profoundly and with all humility, for making a difference in your life. Offer a little act of loving kindness as an act of thanksgiving to your Guru

Meditation on Thanksgiving

The secret of a happy contented life is the attitude of gratitude.

Let us try a simple meditation to cultivate the spirit of thanksgiving, the attitude of gratitude.

Step 1: Let us relax. Relax every muscle, every limb, every nerve in the body. Make it tension-free.

Relax your shoulders. Drop all the weight you are carrying with you – all your burdens, all your problems.

Now, let the mind be free – free from the worries of the past, free from fears for the future.

Live in the present moment – be conscious of the now and here!

Now, let us sit in a comfortable posture so that we will not need to change it for the next ten minutes.

Now, take in three deep breaths. As you breathe deeply, be relaxed.

Breathe in... slowly, evenly, deeply...

Now breathe out... slowly... evenly... completely...

(3 breaths)

Step 2: Now tell yourself, as you breathe in: I am grateful to God for all the abundant blessings He has bestowed on me! I am grateful for my family and friends; I am grateful for my home and its amenities; I am grateful for my career, my studies or my vocation in life.

Say to God: I am grateful for the marvellous mechanism of the human body and the incredible instrument that is the human mind. I am grateful too, for the five senses that enable me to perceive this world, and the power of thinking that makes me what I am – a living, walking, talking, sensitive human being.

I am grateful to God for every breath I take, and the new life, the new energy that each breath brings into my being!

Inhale deeply, feel yourself becoming new and fresh with every breath you take. Express your gratitude to the Almighty for every breath, every second of life that comes as a priceless gift to you from God! (Silence: 1 minute)

Step 3: Now, feel the spirit of thanksgiving flowing through every nerve, every pore of your body. Repeat to yourself the *mantra*: Thank you God! Thank you God! Thank you God! (Silence: 1 minute)

Dwelling on the attitude of gratitude makes us open and receptive to the Lord's blessings. Feel the Lord's richest blessings being showered on you in abundance! Thank Him profoundly for all the gifts you are aware of – and for a thousand others which you have not acknowledged till now! Repeat to yourself the *mantra*: Thank you God! Thank you God! Thank you God! (Silence: 1 minute)

Step 4: Feel the peace and contentment that enter your heart as you repeat the *mantra*: I believe in God's goodness, I believe that he has a plan for me! I am content to let that plan unfold in my life... I am content... I am grateful to God for all His blessings. I am content to accept His will.. I accept, I accept, I accept.... (Silence: 1 minute)

Step 5: Now, let us offer our gratitude to God and the Guru. Visualise yourself before God; visualise yourself at the Lotus Feet of the Master, offering flowers of devotion and gratitude: what can you offer to the Beloved who asks nothing of you? Only this: that you will do what pleases Him most; that you will help everyone, appreciate everyone, and love everyone. And that you will live in the spirit of thanksgiving every day, every hour, every beautiful moment of this life! (Silence: 1 minute)

Count your blessings, keep on thanking the Lord. This induces the marvellous and restful feeling that God is in His Heaven and all is well with this world.

(Silence: 1 minute)

Become aware of the rhythm of your breathing. Open your eyes gently, and feel the positive energy of thanksgiving infusing your body, mind, heart and soul.

Om Shanti! Shanti! Shanti!